Don't Take a Bath on a Friday

Don't Take a Bath on a Friday

Philippine Superstitions and Folk Beliefs

Selected and edited by
Neni Sta. Romana-Cruz

Drawings by
Katti Sta. Ana

Tahanan Books

Manila

Published by Tahanan Books
A division of Tahanan Pacific, Inc.
P.O. Box 9079, MCS Mailing Center
1299 Makati City, Philippines

Designed by Roberto T. Canlas
Printed in the Philippines by Island Graphics
10 9 8 7

National Library of the Philippines
Cataloging-in-Publication Data

Recommended entry:

Don't take a bath on a Friday : Philippine superstitions and folk beliefs / edited by Neni Sta. Romana-Cruz ; drawings by Katti Sta. Ana. – Makati City : Tahanan Books c1996 1 v

1. Superstition – Philippines. I. Cruz, Neni S.R. II. Sta. Ana, Katti.

BF1775 398.41'09599 1996 P963000268
ISBN 971-630-060-3

Contents

For Gilda C. Fernando and Odette Alcantara,
for setting me off on this curiosity,
and for Elfren, Tanya, Roel, and Aina

N.S.R.C.

For my God

K.S.A.

Introduction

I recently found myself preparing for a ceremony that is mandatory prior to building a house in the Philippines. Our contractor and architect gave me a list of prerequisites—the most propitious day and hour to break ground, a white-feathered native chicken to be slaughtered as a peace-offering, and a shovel for the first ceremonial dig. These were mentioned in the same breath as all of the bureaucratic requirements for a building permit!

The ground-breaking ritual, scheduled during the Chinese New Year, began before 8 A.M. It was a curious mix of Catholicism, Chinese traditions, Pinoy folk beliefs, with strong pagan undertones. We made the sign of the cross, and fervently recited our prayers for a successful undertaking. Thereupon the contractor performed the *padugo*, or blood-letting. He slit open the throat of the white chicken, sprinkling drops of blood in the construction area. Then he mercilessly cut its head off, and let it loose for its frenzied dance of death. This was done to appease the gods and the spirits-in-residence who may be offended or disturbed by our intrusion.

When it all was over, I realized just how much my life is governed by the power of unwritten laws.

Superstitions reveal much of what people revere and hold dear. They help us cope with the unknown, the unexplained, and the mysterious. They are widely-held folk beliefs and customs which are often based on personal experiences. They may be founded on scientific facts, opinions, religions, popular practices, or simply, inexplicable coincidences.

Scholars of folklore distinguish between folk beliefs and superstitions. Dr. Damiana Eugenio, who compiled and edited the *Philippine Folk Literature Series*, avoids using the term "superstition." To her the word is associated with ignorance and beliefs which cannot be scientifically proven. She prefers to call them "folk beliefs"—a neutral term that, according to her, emphasizes their basic harmlessness.

The impressive, two-volume scholarly work by Father Francisco Demetrio, S.J., *Encyclopedia of Philippine Folk Beliefs and Customs,* covers about

8,000 folk beliefs and bears witness to over twenty years of fieldwork. I discovered that many such beliefs and customs are adhered to in households known to me, even in the heart of Metro Manila!

It was with great interest that I read through another important source: original manuscripts belonging to the notable American professor, scholar, and anthropologist, Otley H. Beyer, and made available to me through the kindness of Gilda Cordero-Fernando and Odette Alcantara. These were reports written by students from the University of the Philippines on the superstitious beliefs of their own provinces. These manuscripts, painstakingly handwritten on ruled paper now brittle and yellow with age, date back to the 1920s and 30s.

Dr. Beyer wrote that "In a country like the Philippines where people have been isolated in small groups for long periods of time—leading to the development of many differences in language and dialect—it is especially important that collections of the local tales and beliefs should be made for each province and municipality, in order that the world at large may...have access to the interesting lore and popular knowledge preserved in these islands."

Compiling Philippine superstitions for this book was a delightful endeavor. It was a fascinating journey through the complex and mystifying Filipino psyche, as well as a nostalgic return to my childhood.

Many of these superstitions brought back memories of admonitions from *yayas* (nannies), elders, and provincial folk. My holy fear of defying enchanted spirits dictated when I should bathe or comb my hair, and places I had to avoid whenever I played in the garden. Most frightening of all was the belief that I might go insane if I went to bed with wet hair!

Some superstitions leave you in total bewilderment. Taken together, you cannot take a bath in the afternoons, in the evenings, on Sundays, Mondays, Tuesdays, Thursdays, Fridays, on first Fridays, Good Friday, New Year's Day, on the feast of St. Lazarus, on the thirteenth day of every month, during a month with only 30 days, before gambling, when hungry, after eating, after going to church, during holidays, when there is a rainbow, as the moon sets and as the sun rises, during full moons, new moons, and even when the moon wanes and disappears. One might ask if there is any time left to bathe without dire consequences?

Some superstitions I encountered in my research were objectionably sexist. According to one, if a man on an errand meets a girl, his mission will definitely fail! Another, that if a store's first customer for the day is a man, it augurs well for the day's business. In both cases, the reverse is spelled out as a truism.

Perhaps the most meaningful impact that superstitions have on our lives is the glimpse they give us of ourselves and of times past. If only to lead us to a better appreciation of the many facets of the Filipino mystique, rereading these folk beliefs would have served a purpose.

The superstitions included here, nearly two hundred in all, are my personal choices based on their appeal, popularity, and uniqueness.

Whether these superstitions charm or amuse or seem unbelievable today, who among us has the temerity to trifle with luck and taunt fate itself? Chuckle, if you must, over the superstitions in this small book. But don't say I didn't warn you if you fail to heed their advice!

NENI STA. ROMANA-CRUZ
3 MARCH 1996

Love and Marriage

If you want to know beforehand what your lifetime partner will look like, wake up at midnight and look at yourself in the mirror while holding a lighted candle. At first, the image in the mirror will appear to be a skeleton; after five minutes you will see a full view of the person you will marry.

You may give
your sweetheart
a handkerchief
as a gift,
but it will only
make her cry.

When a star appears near a half-moon, it is a sign that young couples are eloping.

Sweethearts should not exchange pointed or sharp objects as gifts, for this will lead to a broken engagement.

The bride- and groom-to-be must avoid traveling before their wedding day to avoid accidents.

The bride-to-be shouldn't try on her wedding dress before the day of the wedding, or the wedding will not take place.

The groom must arrive at the church before the bride to prevent bad luck.

Dropping the wedding ring, or the couple's veil, or *arrhae* during the wedding ceremony, spells unhappiness for the couple.

The groom who sits down ahead of his bride during the wedding ceremony will be a henpecked husband.

IF IT SHOWERS DURING THE WEDDING, IT MEANS PROSPERITY AND HAPPINESS FOR THE COUPLE.

During the wedding ceremony a bride must step on her husband's foot so that both of them will agree on things that they will undertake, and so that her husband will not be cruel to her.

Whoever of the couple stands first after the ceremony, will die ahead of the other.

It is a bad omen for the newlyweds when their parents cry at their wedding.

A bride who cries during the wedding ceremony brings bad luck.

If it rains during the wedding, the couple will have many crybabies.

Throwing rice at the newlyweds will bring them prosperity all their life.

Breaking something during the wedding reception brings good luck to the newlyweds.

Upon entering their new home, both bride and groom should go up the stairs side-by-side, so that neither of them will be superior to the other.

It is bad luck for two siblings to marry within the same year. A remedy for this is to have the sibling who marries later in the year pass the backstairs of the church on the day of the wedding.

A person who habitually sits at the head of the table during meals will never marry.

Women who have moles under their eyes, right where the tears fall, will be widowed.

Removing plates from the table while an unmarried woman is still eating will keep her single all her life.

AN UNWED GIRL WHO FOLLOWS THE FOOTPRINTS OF A NEWLY-WED COUPLE, WILL MARRY SOON.

If a woman is widowed during a new moon, she will surely marry again.

A married woman who wears a pearl ring will cause her husband to commit adultery.

If the husband leaves the house soon after a quarrel, the wife should get his shirt, hang it over the stove, and whip it several times. The husband is certain to come back.

Pregnancy and Childbirth

If a pregnant woman's abdomen is pointed, her baby will be a boy; if it is round, the baby will be a girl.

Give an expectant mother anything she craves for, or she will have a miscarriage.

If a pregnant woman wants to avoid the unpleasant symptoms of pregnancy, she should step over her husband while he's sleeping and all of her symptoms will be transferred to him.

If a pregnant woman eats a fruit from a tree, all the remaining fruits will turn sour.

A pregnant woman who eats twin bananas will give birth to twins. To prevent this, she must split the twin bananas behind her back.

A pregnant woman shouldn't have her picture taken, or her child will die at birth.

Visitors who do not enter the house, but linger at the door instead, will cause a pregnant woman a difficult delivery.

When a woman is about to give birth, place a lighted candle under her bed so that any witches passing by may be seen.

After the baby is delivered, the umbilical cord must be rubbed on the newborn's cheek to produce dimples.

When a baby lies on her stomach for the first time, place a pencil, paper, and a book under her so that she will be intelligent.

Infants and Children

If a baby often holds his feet, it means he wants a younger brother or sister.

Cutting a baby's eyelashes during her first month will make them grow long and beautiful.

An infant must not be kissed when he is sleeping because he will turn naughty when he grows up.

A baby who sucks on her toes means her mother will soon be pregnant again.

Kissing a baby's feet will result in the baby talking back to his parents when he grows up.

A breech baby will bring luck to the family. She will also have the power to remove fish spines stuck in another person's throat by merely touching that person's throat.

The child that cries during his baptism is a sign of prosperity. The harder the child cries, the richer the child will be.

Stepping over a child
will slow his growth.

When a baby is baptized, he should be carried by a person with plenty of coins in his or her pocket. This gives the baby good luck.

When a child is ready to walk, put him on the stairs. Have him step on a plate or anywhere else so long as his feet do not touch the ground first. This is to ensure that he will always find his way home from wherever he may roam.

If a child's baby tooth falls out, throw it up onto the roof so that the rats will find it. When the new tooth grows in, it will be as strong and as powerful as a rat's tooth.

Children should not be allowed to play late in the afternoon when the horizon is yellow-orange, because evil spirits roam around at that time.

Money and Wealth

A person who breaks an egg
and finds two yolks inside, will be rich.

- A white butterfly is a sign of impending wealth.

- A house frequented by black ants means that its owner will be rich.

- A small anthill under the house is a sign of good fortune.

- Don't set your purse or handbag down on the floor, or you will not prosper.

- Never sweep the floor at night, or you'll lose all your wealth.

- Anyone who pays his debts at night will become poor.

- As soon as you see a shooting star, wrap some money in a corner of your handkerchief and play any game of chance, for you are sure to win.

If your palm itches, it means you will soon receive a lot of money.

If you dress up and discover that you are wearing your dress inside out, it means that you are going to receive money shortly.

Always keep a coin inside your suitcase or bag. If you don't spend it, you'll have money throughout the year.

If you find a coin on the road, put it in your purse or pocket. If you never use it, you'll never be short of money.

Give a generous discount to the day's first customer, so that your sales for the day will increase (*buena mano*).

Food and Dining

***A FISH BONE STUCK
IN A PERSON'S THROAT
MAY BE REMOVED BY
BRUSHING A CAT'S TAIL
AGAINST THE PERSON'S NECK.***

If a spoon falls during a meal, you'll be visited by a woman. If it's a fork, it will be a man and if it's a teaspoon, a child.

A woman who switches seats many times during a meal will have many suitors.

If you have to leave the table before finishing your meal in order to go on a trip, turn the plates on the table around so that your trip may be safe.

If you change your permanent place at the family table, the person you marry will have a short life.

Don't put money on the table while you are eating.

The number of persons sitting down to a meal should not add up to 13.

If you eat too many onions, you will become a playboy or playgirl.

Eating ripe papayas everyday controls sexual urges.

When cooking, leave a few grains of rice in the sack and then tie it tightly. This way your guests will not consume all of the food at once.

If you leave some rice in the pot there will always be something in the house to eat.

If you choke briefly at mealtime, someone far away remembers, or is talking about, you.

If a fish bone gets stuck in your throat, don't tell a soul; turn your plate around three times and the bone will disappear.

❧ It's good to use plates when serving food to your visitors. The grace of your guests will remain on the plates and be a blessing to your family.

❧ When a stranger or distant relative arrives in your home, serve him water first so that he brings you only good news.

❧ When dining in the home of strangers, always eat food from the center of the plate. Witches are known to place their powers towards the sides of the plates.

❧ Don't stack your dirty dishes one on top of the other, or it may lead to adultery.

House and Home

Bees found inside the house
will bring fortune and
good luck to its occupants.

- Always begin construction during a full moon.

- The best months for building a house are March, June, July, August, September, and November.

- Never build your house at the end of a dead end road.

- It's bad luck for a house to have thirteen posts.

- When building a house, remember to place certain things under each structural post. Old coins and religious medals will drive away evil spirits and ensure prosperity. Musical score sheets, medals, and coins ensure harmony.

IF YOU WANT TO RID YOUR HOUSE OF BEDBUGS, PLACE SOME ON A PIECE OF PAPER AND THEN LEAVE THEM IN SOMEONE ELSE'S HOUSE. THE BEDBUGS WILL MOVE TO THAT HOUSE.

The number of steps on a staircase should not be in multiples of three. Count off the steps as *oro* (gold), *plata* (silver), and *mata* (death). The last step must not fall on mata.

Always move into a new house on a Wednesday or Saturday.

If you move into a new home one day before the new moon, you'll never go hungry.

The first things one should carry into a new home on moving day are rice and salt.

When moving into a new home, scatter coins in the *sala* (living room) so prosperity will reign.

When doves and pigeons leave a house, it is a sign that there is no harmony there because its owners are quarreling all the time.

If you wish to rid your home of unwanted visitors, secretly sprinkle salt around the house and they will soon depart.

A guest should not leave the house while the family is eating because opening the doors will let out all the family's good fortune.

All windows should be opened on New Year's Day to let God's grace in.

The number of people sleeping in a new house the first night should be the same for nine consecutive days. Otherwise, death will occur.

Illness and Death

Going to bed with wet hair leads to blindness or insanity.

A wound inflicted on Good Friday will take a long time to heal.

It's a good idea to change the name of a sickly child. That way you may be able to fool the spirits who are causing the sickness.

Before you bathe in a spring or river, you must first ask permission from the *engkantos* (spirits who have the power to enchant people) who dwell there. Otherwise you might catch a disease.

Before passing over a small hill, you must first ask permission from the *engkantos* so that you will not get sick.

A lingering black butterfly is a sign that one of your relatives has just died.

- A falling spider that lands on you is an omen that someone close to you will die.

- Do not form groups of three or thirteen, because one among you will die.

- If you dream that one of your teeth is being pulled out, this means that a family member will die.

- Sometimes the soul departs from the body during a deep sleep. Rousing a person at this time might kill him.

- It is said that the soul of the deceased returns on the third, fifth, and seventh days after death.

- Be careful that your tears don't fall on the dead or on the coffin. If they do, the dead person will have a difficult journey to the next world.

If someone sneezes at a wake, pinch him lest he join the dead.

During a wake, never see your visitors off at the door of the chapel or funeral parlor.

Always carry the coffin out of the house head first. This prevents the soul of the dead from coming back.

During the funeral march, a man whose wife is pregnant should not carry the casket. Before going home he should light up a cigarette from a fire at the cemetery gate in order to shake off the spirits of the dead.

A widow who caresses her dead husband's face is sure to remarry.

Digging a hole larger than the coffin will cause an immediate relative to join the deceased in the grave.

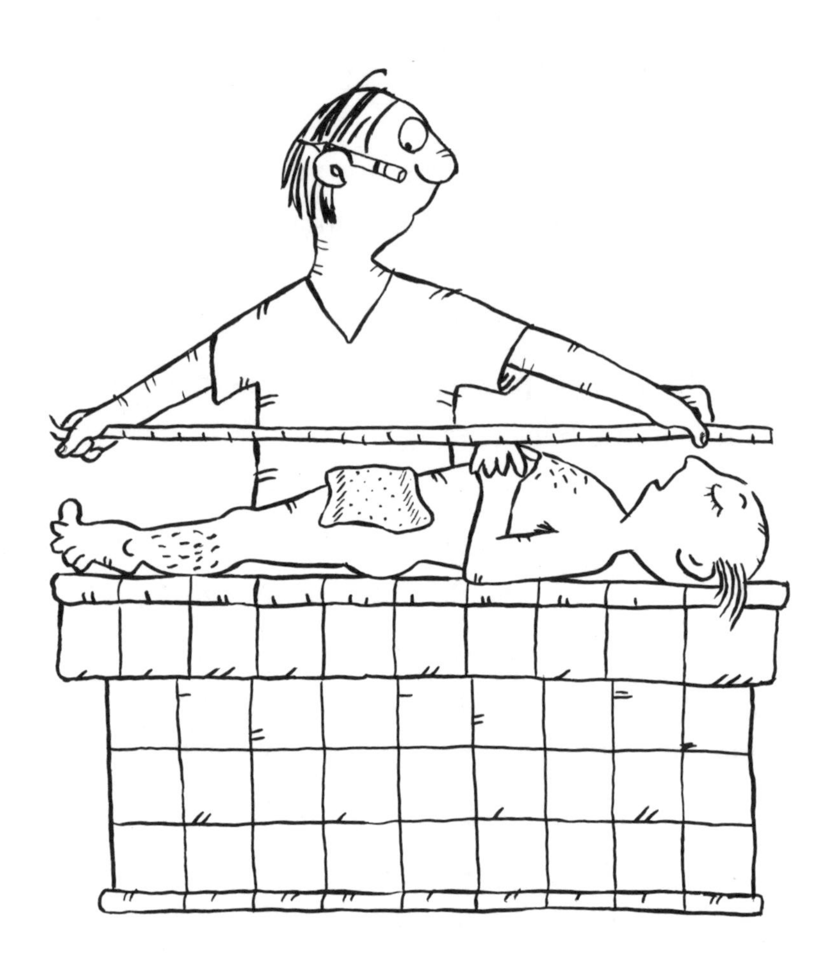

The coffin should be built to fit the exact measurement of the corpse. Otherwise a family member of the deceased will soon die.

After the coffin has been lowered to the grave, all family members should take a handful of soil, spit on it, and throw it in the grave. Doing so will not only bury any evil left behind by the deceased, but lessen the burden of grief on the family as well.

After the funeral service, do not go home directly so that the spirit of the dead person will not follow you to your house.

Never let a child step over an open grave lest the spirit of the dead visit that child.

When a tree that was planted at the same time that a child was born dies, the child will die also.

Do not sweep the house until after the burial.

Give away your black dresses after one year of mourning to prevent another death in the family.

Colors and Numbers

When three people pose for a photo, the one in the middle will be the first to die.

- A red car is prone to accidents.

- A person with dark-colored gums is said to be jealous.

- A person's favorite color reveals facets of her personality—yellow for jealousy, red for energy, white for peacefulness, green for optimism, and blue for loneliness.

- If you dream of your friends wearing white suits, it means that they will get married.

- If you wear black clothes even though you are not in mourning, one of your relatives will die.

- A person with two or more cowlicks is said to be mischievous.

- Tragic events happen in three's.

A single rumble of thunder announces the death of a prominent person.

Giving birth consecutively to three children of the same sex will bring good luck to the parents.

Gamblers who encounter the number 7 will lose.

Breaking a mirror on a Friday brings seven years of bad luck.

The numbers 3, 5, and 9 are unlucky.

Thirteen is both a lucky and an unlucky number.

Do not choose the number 22 for a wedding date. Since this number is in the "kneeling" position, it will not give the couple prosperity.

If the number of letters comprising the names of both husband and wife add up to 30 or more, it means good luck.

A person who dreams of numbers will win the lottery.

Animals

If a chicken walks in the rain,
the rain will stop.

When winged ants (*gamo-gamo*) fly at night, it is a sign of impending rain.

If frogs croak in the summertime, it is a sign of the coming rain.

If you bathe a cat, lightning will strike you.

Don't speak ill of mice, lest they harm you. Refer to them as *mabait* (good).

A cat wiping its face is a sign that a visitor is coming.

A hen clucking at dawn is a sign that an unmarried woman is pregnant.

When dogs howl at night, it means that evil spirits are lurking about.

When dogs howl at night, turn your shoes over to keep death from stealing into them.

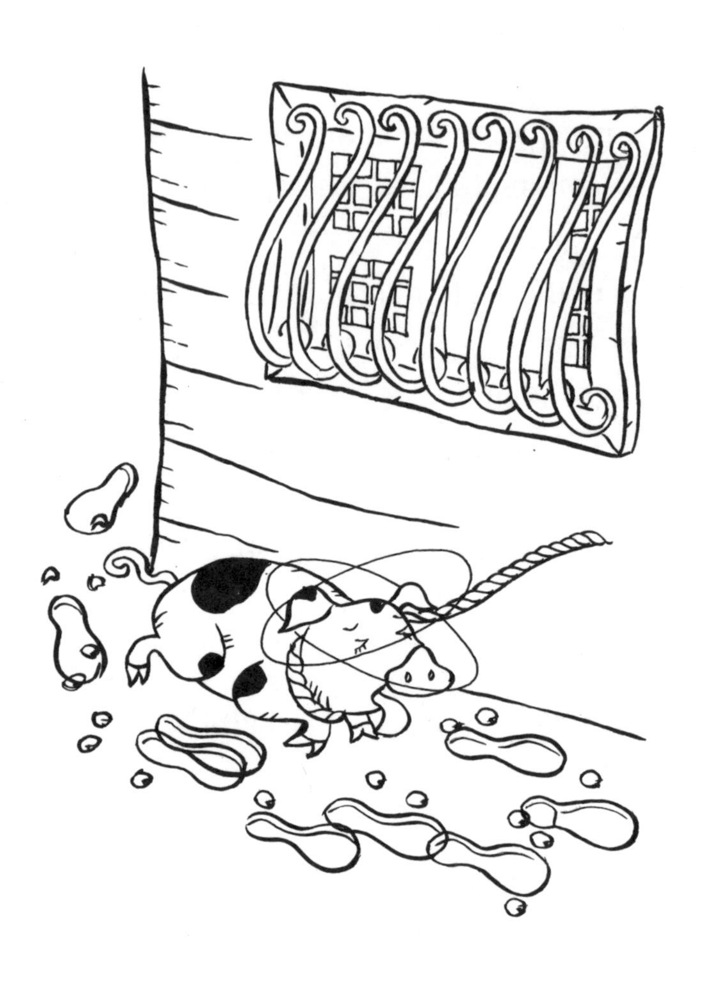

**AFTER BUYING A PIGLET,
WALK IT AROUND YOUR HOUSE
SEVEN TIMES SO IT WILL NOT GO ASTRAY.**

When a house lizard makes a lot of noise, expect a letter or a visitor.

A spider seen at night is a sign of good fortune, while a spider seen during the day is a sign of misfortune.

If a spider falls from his web and fails to climb back up, it signifies sorrow for the family. But if it falls and climbs back up again, it means that happiness is at hand.

If a gambler meets a lizard on the way to the cockpit, it's a sign of bad luck. If he meets a snake, it's good luck.

Telltale Signs

When a sleeping adult laughs, it means that a relative will die. When a sleeping child laughs, it means that the angels are playing with him.

A person with a mole on her foot is a born adventurer.

A person with a mole on his face will be successful in business.

A person with a mole in the middle of her nose will be rich but unhappy.

A person with a mole in his eye is attractive to the opposite sex.

A mole on the hand signifies wealth or thievery.

A mole on one's back is a sign of laziness.

A person with big ears will have a long life.

Men with hairy chests are playboys.

Women who have wide hips will bear many children.

People with naturally curly hair are moody or ill-tempered.

People who have eyebrows that almost meet get jealous easily.

If you see an eyelash falling, it means you will receive a letter.

A person with lines running from the palm of his hand to his fingers is successful in business.

People whose teeth are spaced far apart are liars.

If a person bites her tongue, it means somebody is thinking of or talking about her.

When a person forgets what he wants to say, it means that the devil has snatched his words.

A woman who combs her hair with her back towards the door is a sign of infidelity.

If all the matches should fall out of a matchbox, you'll have an unexpected visitor.

A month that starts on a Friday will be full of accidents.

A person who always uses a bandage on Fridays is a witch.

The appearance of a comet is an omen of war, famine, or sickness.

Bad Luck, Good Luck

A black cat crossing your path is a bad omen.

The black cat is a demon in disguise.

Encountering a yellow butterfly will bring you good luck.

If you are awakened by chirping birds at dawn, luck awaits you.

Dreaming of fish, trees, or snakes means good fortune, money, or happiness.

Lying down with your feet facing the door will bring you an early death.

Adorning your dress with pearls means you will shed many tears.

If a brown butterfly enters your house, you will lose money.

Do not mend your clothes while wearing them, or harm will befall you.

- Stepping on a pillow brings misfortune.

- A person who is headed somewhere should not proceed with her journey if she trips on something after leaving the house. Something terrible will happen to her.

- If you sit on your bag while traveling, you will not reach your destination.

A person who breaks a mirror faces seven years of bad luck

At the stroke of midnight on New Year's Eve, eat twelve grapes which represent the twelve months of the year. This will ensure money and good luck throughout the year.

Whistling at night invites evil spirits.

Wearing a diamond protects the bearer from evil-minded people.

Superstitions and Sundry

Don't take a bath on a Friday. Don't take a bath in the afternoon. Don't take a bath in the evening. Don't take a bath on Sundays, Mondays, Tuesdays, Thursdays, and Fridays. Don't take a bath on a first Friday. Don't take a bath on Good Friday. Don't take a bath on New Year's Day. Don't take a bath on the feast day of St. Lazarus. Don't take a bath on the thirteenth day of every month. Don't take a bath during a month composed of only 30 days. Don't take a bath when hungry. Don't take a bath after eating. Don't take a bath before gambling. Don't take a bath after going to church. Don't take a bath during holidays. Don't take a bath when there's a rainbow. Don't take a bath during a full moon.

Cry tonight and you'll be happy tomorrow.

Don't gamble if you've just had a haircut, for you are certain to lose.

Never give a pair of shoes away for free. Either throw the shoes up in the air and let the prospective owner pick them up, or let him or her buy it for five centavos.

Don't comb your hair at night, lest you become bald, orphaned, or widowed. But if you must comb at night, bite the tip of the comb first.

Avoid recurring dreams by turning your pillow upside down.

Always sleep facing east, or you will not face a bright future.

Sitting on a pile of books will make a person dull.

❧ If a person sleeps on her books, she will have a good memory.

❧ Whistling while flying a kite will cause the wind to blow.

❧ Before throwing hot water onto the ground, give a warning to the elves. When harmed, they may retaliate by making you sick.

❧ Before stepping over an anthill, first ask to be excused. Otherwise a spirit may play tricks on you.

❧ Carry a piece of ginger on your body when you visit places not frequented by others, so that the evil spirits of that place will not harm you.

❧ If you walk in the forest, rub your feet with garlic to prevent animals from harming you.

After studying at night, place the book you've been studying under your pillow, and you will retain what you have read.

Do not harm or cut down a *balete* tree because it is the dwelling place of fairies and enchanted spirits.

Don't go out on Holy Thursday and Good Friday, for evil fairies are roaming around to hurt people.

Don't whistle or sing in the forest lest the *engkantos* imitate you and cause you to fall ill.

When walking with your friends, especially at night, always travel in a group made up of an even number. If it's an odd number, one of you will be taken away by the spirits to make the number even.

Washed clothes should be taken from the clothesline at night, lest they be stolen and worn by dwarfs.

If someone sneezes while you are about to leave your house, postpone your trip or something bad will happen.

Whatever you do or feel on New Year's Day will continue the rest of the year.

Better to find money on New Year's Day than spend it.

Jumping on Easter morning hastens growth and makes a person taller.

When the bells ring on Easter Sunday, shout at the top of your lungs and you will have a long life.

To determine who stole a lost item, write down the names of all the suspects on sheets of paper and boil them. The name on the sheet of paper that is not erased is the guilty person.

To prevent rain, take ashes from the kitchen and spread them over your yard.

ꟹ To overcome stage fright when speaking in public, tuck a one-centavo coin inside the shoes you are wearing.

ꟹ Don't cut your nails at night or on Tuesdays, Wednesdays, and Fridays.

ꟹ If you happen to get lost, invert your clothes and you'll find your way.

Bibliography

Alba, Rene, ed. *Filipino Customs and Traditions.* Caloocan City: Mizrack Publications.

Beyer, Otley H. Reports written by students from the University of the Philippines for their anthropology course, 1924, 1925, 1926, and 1930. Odette Alcantara Collection.

Coffin, Tristram P. and Hennig Coppen, eds. *Folklore in America.* New York: Doubleday & Co., 1966.

de Guzman, Jovita Varias and Rodolfo R. Varias. *Psychology of Filipinos.* Manila: Vilfran, 1965.

Demetrio, Fr. Francisco, S.J. *Encyclopedia of Philippine Folk Beliefs and Customs.* Vols. I and II. Cagayan de Oro City: Xavier University, 1991.

Galang, Zoilo, ed. *Encyclopedia of the Philippines.* Vol. I, *Literature*, by Exequiel Floro. Manila: McCullough Printing Co., 1950.

Perl, Lila. *Don't Sing Before Breakfast, Don't Sleep in the Moonlight: Everyday Superstitions and How They Began.* New York: Clarion Books, 1988.

Sarnoff, Jane and Reynold Puffins. *Take Warning!* New York: Charles Scribner's Sons, 1978.

About the Author

Neni Sta. Romana-Cruz is a respected figure in the field of children's literature. She won the 1993 National Book Award for Children's Literature for her book *Why the Piña Has a Hundred Eyes and Other Classic Philippine Folk Tales About Fruits,* published by Tahanan Books for Young Readers. Her biography of Gabriela Silang, written for Tahanan's Great Lives series, received a 1992 National Book Award citation for excellence. She also wrote a collection of essays titled *Sundays of Our Lives.*

Ms. Cruz has chaired the Philippine Board on Books for Young People and is a children's book critic and free-lance journalist. She currently teaches writing to talented elementary school students and heads the Children's Media Center at the International School Manila.

After graduating *cum laude* from St. Scholastica's College, Ms. Cruz pursued a master's degree in English literature from Ateneo University.

She lives with her husband, Elfren, and their children, Tanya, Roel, and Aina in Parañaque, Metro Manila.

About the Artist

Katti Sta. Ana received her bachelor's degree in fine arts from the University of the Philippines, where she majored in painting. She was a finalist at the 1995 Philip Morris Philippine Art Awards. Her first picture book for children is *Ang Prinsesang Ayaw Matulog.* Ms. Sta. Ana regularly illustrates for *Mirror Weekly,* and is a member of Ang Ilustrador ng Kabataan, an organization of young artists devoted to children's book illustration.

She lives in Marikina.